The Threefold Way of Saint Francis

Murray Bodo, O.F.M.

Paulist Press

New York/Mahwah, New Jersey

Cover/book design and interior illustrations by Nicholas T. Markell.

Library of Congress Cataloging-in-Publication Data

Bodo, Murray.
    The threefold way of Saint Francis / Murray Bodo.
       p.   cm. — (IlluminationBooks)
    Includes bibliographical references.
    ISBN 0-8091-4003-9 (alk. paper)
    1. Francis, of Assisi, Saint, 1182–1226. 2. Spirituality—Catholic Church—History of doctrines—Middle Ages, 600–1500. 3. Catholic Church—Doctrines—History. I. Title. II. Series.

BX4700.F6 B63 2000
248.4′82—dc21

                                    00-044140

Published by Paulist Press
997 Macarthur Boulevard
Mahwah, New Jersey 07430

www.paulistpress.com

Printed and bound in the
United States of America

Contents

IlluminationBooks

A Foreword

When this series was launched in 1994, I wrote that Illumination-Books were conceived to "bring to light wonderful ideas, helpful information, and sound spirituality in concise, illustrative, readable, and eminently practical works on topics of current concern."

In keeping with this premise, among the first books were offerings by well-known authors Joyce Rupp *(Little Pieces of Light...Darkness and Personal Growth)* and Basil Pennington *(Lessons from the Monastery That Touch Your Life)*. In addition, there were titles by up-and-coming authors and experts in the fields of spirituality and psychology.

These books covered a wide array of topics: joy, controlling stress and anxiety, personal growth, discernment, caring for others, the mystery of the Trinity, celebrating the woman you are, and facing your own desert experiences.

The continued goal of the series is to provide great ideas, helpful steps, and needed inspiration in small volumes. Each of the books offers a new opportunity for the reader to explore possibilities and embrace practicalities that can be employed in everyday life. Thus, among the new and noteworthy themes for readers to discover are these: how to be more receptive to the love in our lives, simple ways to structure a personal day of recollection, a creative approach to enjoy reading sacred scriptures, and spiritual and psychological methods of facing discouragement.

Like the IlluminationBooks before them, forthcoming volumes are meant to be a source of support—without requiring an inordinate amount of time or prior preparation. To this end, each small work stands on its own. The hope is that the information provided not only will be nourishing in itself but also will encourage further exploration in the area.

When we view the world through spiritual eyes, we appreciate that sound knowledge is really useful only when it can set the stage for *metanoia*, the conversion of our hearts. Each of the IlluminationBooks is designed to contribute in some small but significant way to this process. So, it is with a sense of hope and warm wishes that I offer this particular title and the rest of the series to you.

–*Robert J. Wicks*

General Editor, IlluminationBooks

Introduction

*S*t. Francis has lived inside of me for almost sixty years. He walks my inner landscape, barefoot, unkempt, his threadbare habit girded with a plain woolen cord, his cowl crushed from sleeping in the woods, a rock for a pillow. He is a knight-errant, a troubadour, a poor fool for the Poor Christ. Il Poverello, Francesco, the saint of Assisi.

Like Don Quixote de La Mancha, he is both idealistic dreamer enthralled with his Dulcinea, the Lady Poverty, and equally the Shakespearean fool who mocks the values of those who put their trust in sword and money and social position. He walks the geography of my soul

looking like a beggar but joyfully and with princely bearing because he walks in the footsteps of his liege-lord, Jesus Christ. His poor tunic and beggar's bowl mimic the trappings of chivalry and knighthood, for he carries his bowl like Lancelot's lance; he rides the merest peasant's donkey like the sleekest steed. He makes of Assisi, Camelot, and of the lepers' swamp below the city, Paradise. The way forward is backward to Paradise; the way up to heaven is down to the poor, the despised, the marginalized of this world.

This Francis, this stigmatic, bearing the wounds of Christ, prays with hands and feet and side afire with love in the visitable place within which is the soul. Wherever I go, wherever I am, I visit St. Francis within to help me see aright what I see outside. Though I stumble, I'm drawn to the way he walks in Jesus' footsteps. He mediates my otherwise too serious, too stiff trudging of the Way of the Cross. Francis turns asceticism into a merry pilgrimage of fools and lovers and singers who chant antiphonally with him, "May the fiery and honey-sweet power of your love, O Lord, wean me from all things under heaven, so that I may die for love of your love, who deigned to die for love of my love."[1]

Such is the landscape within that I retreat to in order to see as blessed what otherwise would seem a world gone mad with power and greed, with sensationalism and exaggerated nationalism, with instant gratification, with exclusion and prejudice, hatred and war. Through the eyes of St. Francis all is lit with a light from within, for everything, even death, is ultimately made of God's love, redeemed by God's Word, inspirited by God's own Spirit.

The Franciscan charism is to reveal to the world its essentially good and holy face, so often masked with false faces that twist God's image into something unrecognizable except to the saints among us who remind us, as St. Francis does, that we are more good than bad. "Buon giorno, buona gente," *Good* morning, *good* people, St. Francis sang through the streets of the small mountain village of Poggio Bustone, sang with gusto and joy, for there on the mountain above the Rieti Valley, Francis came to accept God's love for him, came to acknowledge for the first time that he was forgiven, that God loved him even when he was in sin, that all his sins were now forgiven, simply by his being humble enough to receive God's forgiveness. There he came to know in prayer that God loved him and all other creatures and all of creation with an everlasting love. He became the face that was there all along, even when in despair he believed his sins were too great for God to forgive them.

My own Franciscan face was dramatically revealed to me twenty years ago as I sat in the office of Dr. Karl Menninger, cofounder of the Menninger Institute in Topeka, Kansas. I had journeyed there to interview him for a magazine article that never materialized, though the effect of that encounter is written on my soul as indelibly as my prayer encounters with St. Francis.

I remember thinking that Kansas was not a place I'd been to; it was a state I'd driven through on my way somewhere else. Yet here I was in Kansas, driving through Emporia to Topeka, about an hour's drive north. The landscape was familiar; I'd seen it from the windows of a Santa Fe train many times as a young teenager going back and forth from New Mexico to the seminary in Cincinnati, Ohio.

I drove onto Commercial Street, Emporia's main drag, and every movie and image I'd seen of middle America opened up before me. There was the broad, empty look up the street with the railroad tracks cutting through the middle of town, their gates poised ominously in air. The voice on the radio droned on in a tired, matter-of-fact tone.

The wind was blowing as it often was when I crossed Kansas, and the melancholy wail of one of the west-bound freight trains made this prairie town seem abandoned and isolated; a feeling of loneliness crept into my bones. I drove on through Emporia and out into the farm country with its rich, black overturned soil. I thought of the homesteaders and their 160 acres and the pain and worry of waiting for rain and the ones who didn't make it and the abandoned frame farmhouses and the dreams that blew away in the Kansas wind.

I headed north toward Topeka and the Menninger Clinic—a magic name for me—and now this unexpected opportunity to interview Karl Menninger, the grand old man of American psychiatry. With his father and brother and later his son and nephews, Karl Menninger had helped put Topeka on the map as more than just a stop on the Atchison, Topeka and Santa Fe Railroad.

The drive was a pleasant one, and my excitement heightened as I began to see signs labeled "Topeka." I had seen the name hundreds of times on trains passing through my hometown of Gallup, New Mexico. Now Topeka was important again and growing up got mixed up in my mind with growing toward Topeka and what it stood for in mental health. For fifteen years I'd read and reread Karl Menninger's *The Theory of Psychoanalytic Technique*, and just recently I'd read his book *Whatever Became of Sin?* Maybe he could tell me.

I drove onto the east campus of the clinic grounds up the hill toward the Tower building. I was early with anticipation and nervousness over meeting and talking with this great man. I remembered something he wrote in his book *The Vital Balance*. I stopped the car and looked up the heavily underlined passage.

> Besieged by multitudes of...petitioners, often with gifts in their hands, the doctor—knowing his limitations—must try to be patient, kind, merciful, and honest. But simultaneously he must try to be "objective," to be influenced in his acts and words only by "scientific facts." The desire to bring comfort, the need to earn one's living, the suppressed longing for prestige and popularity, the honest conviction of the efficacy of a pill or a program, sympathy for the pleading sufferer—all these throw themselves upon the scales in the moment of decision. Thus every physician in the world has heard the devil whispering, "Command that these stones become bread....All these things I will give if you fall down and worship." And sometimes he falls down. He commits the sin of presumptuousness, *hubris*. He abandons a first principle of medical art and medical science—humility.[2]

I knew I would like a man who wrote like that. And when I shook his hand, I was not disappointed. His hand was warm as he led me to a chair beside his semicircular desk. He looked at me kindly and put me at ease with "You have a real Franciscan face." He patted my hand again and apologized for his tiredness and his hand hot with fever. He had come down with a touch of the flu but didn't want to disappoint me by canceling our appointment. He had become his own words:

> The world's greatest lovers have not been Don Juans and Casanovas, but Schweitzers, Gandhis, Helen Kellers, and such saints as Francis of Assisi....What psychoanalysis showed was that true love is more concerned about the welfare of the one loved than with its own immediate satisfactions, that it is free from jealousy, boastfulness, arrogance, and rudeness; that it can bear all things, hope, and endure. So said St. Paul. So said Freud.[3]

And so, what I observed was Karl Menninger, an octogenarian, selflessly giving his time to an ordinary Franciscan priest.

We talked at length but I remember little of what he said, except his very first words, "You have a real Franciscan face." No one had ever said that to me before. He knew, wise old man that he was, that no matter what we spoke of, what questions I asked, I would really be saying, "I hope you like me, I hope this interview is going well, I hope I'm okay in your eyes." And so like one who listens between the lines at what is there but not said, he answered the real question, "Yes, you have a real Franciscan face."

This passing remark has remained with me. It is a gift from Karl Menninger that enables me and reminds me to give that gift to others: Everyone wants to know if she or he is good, is beautiful, has something to give. The Franciscan gift to them is affirmation of the light, manifest or hidden, of their true face.

As I was leaving Karl Menninger, never to see him again, he asked me to try something. "When you change planes at O'Hare Airport, you'll probably have a serious walk to your connection. Instead of setting your teeth and walking determinedly to your plane, try to make eye contact with as many people as you can, loving them with your eyes."

What may have sounded corny or sentimental coming from anyone else, rang instead like an admonition St. Francis would have given me. And so, tired and almost running to make my connection at O'Hare, I tried to make eye contact, whispered to each face, "I love you." It made a difference to me, lifted my heart, and apparently did the same for some of those I passed, who halted briefly on their headlong rush and turned to look at me again as perhaps someone they knew, someone remembered. Some even smiled.

The Francis who lives in me, the Francis of Poggio Bustone, enabled me to hear the words of Karl Menninger and act upon them. They seemed right. They seemed Franciscan. They rang true to the Francis I visit in prayer.

When Francis composed his penultimate Rule of 1221, he wrote these words that remind me of the effect

Dr. Karl, as he was affectionately called, had upon me. Both Dr. Karl's and Francis's words turned me outward from excessive introspection.

> All good belongs
> To the Lord who is God Most High and Supreme
> Every good is God's.
> So let us thank God
> from whom all good things come.
> All honor and reverence,
> all thanks and glory
> may God have and be given and receive,
> the One who is the Highest, the Supreme,
> who alone is true God,
> for every good is God's
> who alone is good.
> And when we see or hear
> someone speak or do evil
> or blaspheme God,
> let us speak and do what is good
> and praise God,
> who is blessed forever. Amen.[4]

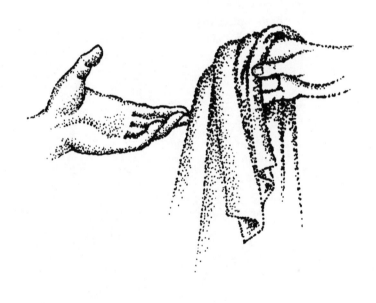

Chapter One
Embracing

Who is the man behind these marvelous words? His name was Francesco, Francis, the son of Pietro Bernardone, the cloth merchant. He was an Assisian, a man of the Middle Ages, who lived from 1182 to 1226. And yet he continues to speak to something deep inside of us who are living in the third millennium. Why is that? Is it his joy, his devotion to Lady Poverty, his embracing the lepers, his love of nature and all created things, or all of these and something more besides? I believe the reason St. Francis continues to attract us today is his passionate love of God made manifest to him in Christ. This love led him to live the gospel and to follow in the footsteps of Christ so wholeheartedly that he became a living prayer. From this love-that-is-prayer and prayer-that-is-love flows everything we find attractive in the Little Poor Man of Assisi.

How then did this divine love affair begin? Francis was one day engaged in his father's cloth merchant trade when a poor man came into the shop begging alms for the love of God. Francis brushed him aside because he was absorbed in selling a piece of cloth. But when the beggar left the shop, Francis, who unlike his father was generous and open-handed by nature, was filled with remorse and ran from the shop looking for the man, promising himself that he would never again refuse an alms begged for the love of God.

This incident caused Francis to experience a closeness to God. He became more reflective, and this meditative mood was reinforced shortly afterward when, as a newly recruited knight, Francis was taken prisoner in a skirmish between Assisi and its rival city of Perugia. He spent a year in prison and there he befriended a young nobleman the other prisoners shunned because he was offensive and uncouth. Again Francis experienced, in the embrace of a rejected person, a closeness to God.

When he was released from prison and came home, he fell into a long illness from which he emerged even more sober and inward looking. The world had lost its splendor for him, and he tried to recapture the old enthusiasm by once more going off to war as a knight. Because Francis's father was wealthy, he was able to purchase the finest armor and horse; but when he met a poor knight along the road, he was moved to exchange his rich attire for the shoddy raiment of the impoverished knight. Again he felt God drawing near, and that evening he had a dream in which God told him to return to Assisi, where he would be told what to do.

So Francis turned his back on war and began a vigil of prayer in a lonely cave on Mt. Subasio, the mountain that towers over Assisi. He would enter the cave each day for prayer and come out at the end of the day to return to his father's house. Then one day, when he was on his way home, he met a leper on the road. Francis had always feared lepers and was nauseated even by the mere sight of them. But when he saw this leper, he suddenly realized he'd been able to pray in the cave because God had drawn near to him for embracing those whom others had rejected and whom he himself had previously found repulsive. And so he jumped off his horse, went over to the leper, and not only gave him money, but embraced him. And when the young Francis turned to leave, he looked back, and there was no one on the road. Francis knew then that once again he had embraced Christ; and because he had, he would continue to be able to hear Christ in prayer.

This conviction was made clear to him a few days later as he was praying in the little tumbled-down chapel of San Damiano. The crucifix that hung above the altar suddenly began to speak and Francis heard: "Francis, go and repair my house which, as you see, is falling into ruin." Francis was so stunned he took the request literally and began immediately to beg stones to repair the church of San Damiano.

Actually what the Crucified Christ was speaking of was the Catholic Church itself, and the way it was to be repaired was by Francis's continued embracing of the poor, the rejected, the real and symbolic lepers of his time. And that is what happened, for the rebuilding of San Damiano changed Francis's whole life. He became a beggar of stones, he was disowned by his father and in turn renounced his father publicly before the Bishop of Assisi. Then he went to live with the lepers, and there he found God once and for all.

Now what could all this possibly have to say to us today? And how can this man who lives with lepers be the same man we see on bird baths all over the world, the joyful troubadour of God, the Knight of Lady Poverty? It's all very simple, really; for we intuitively know that God still dwells where Francis found him.

Deep down we all know where that is. "For I was hungry," says Jesus, "and you gave me food; I was thirsty and you gave me drink; I was a stranger and you made me welcome; naked and you clothed me, sick and you visited me, in prison and you came to me" (Matt 25:35-37).

Furthermore, in running from his father's shop to give alms to the beggar, in embracing the leper, in giving his armor to the poor knight, in befriending the obnoxious nobleman in prison, Francis was not only embracing Christ, but he was embracing that part of himself that he'd not yet come to accept. For if there is someone I can't embrace, could it be that it is because he or she reminds me of some part of myself, or some fear in myself I haven't come to terms with? It is only charity, love, that overcomes fear, and charity begins when I embrace in others what I'm afraid to embrace in myself. I must love my neighbor as I would want to be loved, and if I do that, then in the process I find myself in the embrace of Christ himself. I discover that I am loved by God just as I am, and from that discovery comes all my joy, for I begin to embrace others as God embraced me. In his Last Testament St. Francis writes, "For I, being in sins, thought it bitter to look at lepers, and the Lord himself led me among them, and I worked mercy with them. And when I left their company, I realized that what had seemed bitter to me, had been turned into sweetness of soul and body."[5]

It is interesting that St. Francis uses the word *mercy* rather than *pity*. Not, "I had pity on them," as some erroneous translations have it, but "I worked mercy with them." Pity is condescending, paternalistic, a need to be needed in order to be superior, and makes the other subservient to one's own "goodness." Mercy, on the other hand, is compassion, which means literally, "suffering with," a solidarity with, a sharing in the mercy the "sufferer" is already practicing by letting one share his or her world. Francis learned from his own experience that compassion brings near the God who may seem far away.

What is more, the embrace of our own "lepers" frees us to embrace all of creation, as well, even that from which we might feel alienated. And that is why Francis is the great lover of nature who speaks to birds and animals and holds in his arms everything that is. As the poet Rainer Maria Rilke once wrote:

> But fear of the inexplicable has not alone impoverished the existence of the individual; the relationship between one human being and another has also been cramped by it....And only if we arrange our life by that principle which counsels us that we must always hold to the difficult, then that which now seems to us the most alien will become what we most trust and find most faithful. How should we be able to forget those ancient myths that are at the beginning of all peoples, the myths about dragons that at the last moment turn into princesses; perhaps all the dragons of our lives are princesses who are only waiting to see us once beautiful and brave. Perhaps everything terrible is in its deepest being something helpless that wants help from us.[6]

Francis named the dragon-become-princess Lady Poverty. Because he was steeped in the tradition of the troubadours and the songs and stories of King Arthur and the Knights of the Round Table, Lady Poverty is for Francis like the Lady of the Castle for whom the knight performs his deeds of derring-do. She is the symbolic Bride of Jesus Christ, because as Dante points out she alone joins him on the cross.

From all this, then, St. Francis emerges with a threefold way to God which is his preamble and precondition for anyone wishing to begin a spiritual, interior life.

St. Francis gives us no treatise on interiority, but he does show us three loves that are one, single love of God, and this trinitarian embrace will teach us how to pray, as well: I love God through loving others, through loving myself, and through loving nature. And the way I have learned to love these three is the way I will pray. How I love and the extent that I love teaches me how to pray, gives voice to my endeavor to embrace God. For prayer is essentially the same action, directed toward the God I cannot see, as the loving embrace of what I can see.

In other words, it takes the same kind of faith to believe I am talking with God and that God does hear, as it does to believe I will find God when I embrace what I mistakenly find repulsive, whether in other people, in myself, or in nature. That is the secret of our love for St. Francis: We see in him someone whose whole life is an unsentimental love that embraces what most people mistake for something ugly. And in that embrace God comes to St. Francis, God whom we, too, long for, whom we, too, want to adore in heartfelt prayer. And it is all summed up in the anonymous prayer the whole world has come to associate with Francis of Assisi:

> Lord, make me an instrument of your peace.
> Where there is hatred, let me sow love;
> where there is injury, pardon;
> where there is doubt, faith;
> where there is despair, hope;
> where there is darkness, light;
> and where there is sadness, joy.

O Divine Master, grant that I may not so much
        seek
to be consoled as to console,
to be understood as to understand,
to be loved as to love.

For it is in giving that we receive,
it is in pardoning that we are pardoned,
and it is in dying that we are born to eternal life.

Chapter Two

Integrating

*H*ow, then, are the three ways of St. Francis–love of self, love of others and love of nature–made practical in our day to day living?

Let me begin with a poem by Emily Dickinson.

Some keep the Sabbath going to Church—
I keep it staying at Home—
With a Bobolink for a Chorister—
And an Orchard, for a Dome—
Some keep the Sabbath in Surplice—
I just wear my Wings—
And instead of tolling the Bell, for Church,

Our little Sexton—sings.
God preaches, a noted Clergyman—
And the sermon is never long
So instead of getting to Heaven, at last—
I'm going, all along.[7]

I'm sure you can see that in some ways this is a subversive poem, and in others it is a concrete illustration of that integration and joy that is essential to all spirituality. The point of the poem is not that we stop going to church or being religious; rather the poem exposes the hypocrisy of those who go to church because it is the socially chic thing to do, or in order to be seen, or to feel important and good, or to invest more importance in a noted clergyperson than in the God the clergy are supposed to preach and model in their own lives. The poem also satirizes that false spirituality that denigrates creation, rejects the present world in order to get to heaven. The narrator of the poem states in the last two lines her own spirituality: "So instead of getting to Heaven, at last—/I'm going, all along." That is because the narrator has embraced and integrated God's creation and her own body (which she has adorned with wings) into her keeping Sabbath. And because she has, her heaven is not only a destination, but the going there is itself a heaven of praise and celebration.

This poem is really about integration: the integration of spirituality and daily life. It is about the importance of integrating our journey to God. Unless we so unify our lives that they are a simple, joyful going to God, like lives of the early followers of St. Francis, there is a split, a kind of schizophrenia between our day-to-day living and our so-called spiritual life. If I am always doing things in order to get to heaven, I have failed to make my life a joyful "going all along." I have not embraced my getting there as lovingly as I have embraced my final destination.

St. Francis knew well this kind of split between matter and spirit. He grew up in Assisi, one of 500 towns that were influenced by the Albigensian heresy. The Albigensians, who take their name from their place of origin in Alba, France, believed that matter was created by an evil god, and the spirit by a good god. They believed, as well, that in the beginning the evil god burst into the realm of light and led angelic persons away from the good god. Then in the material world the evil god forces spirits into corporeal bodies as into a prison. The good god in turn permits this as a punishment for their infidelity. Satan is the evil god, and the good god is Yahweh of the Hebrew Bible; and therefore the Albigensians reject the Old Testament and embrace only the New Testament of Jesus Christ.

In the Christology of the Albigensians the good god decides to liberate spirit from matter so he sends his son who is higher than angels but is still a creature. He is Wisdom but is still subordinate to the good god. Christ is not the Incarnate Son of God because if he has taken on a real body, he would be subject to the evil god. So Jesus appears in a make-believe body. His mother Mary is also angelic; she gives birth to Jesus through the ear. Albigensian Christology is a form of gnosticism whereby the word spoken to Mary gives birth through her consciousness to a Word clothed with an illusory body. Therefore, it is the word that is important: the words of Jesus save us, not the passion, death and resurrection of the God-man.

These are the attitudes and beliefs that informed the young Francis, and his conversion consists in a dramatic metanoia, a turning about of attitude and belief, whereby the Incarnate Son of God, Jesus Christ, is the very center and love of his life. He embraces lepers, who were perceived by those imbued with Albigensian attitudes as images of the real evil of matter; he embraces the sacramentality of the Catholic Church which anoints matter as the most important vehicle of grace: the water of baptism, the oil of anointing, the bread and wine of Eucharist, the consummation of married love. Francis also enters into all of creation and praises God through, with, for, and in creatures. In a sense, then, Francis's conversion and subsequent life in God was an anti-Albigensian statement.

It is extraordinary how persistent Albigensian attitudes are throughout history. They are present in the Manichaeism of the time of St. Augustine, and later in Jansenism, and even in some of our contemporary puritanical attitudes. There are still those who look upon the body as evil, who view the whole spiritual struggle as an attempt to free the soul from the "dirty" body. They are suspect of the human and trust only the spiritual. They look upon sanctification as something they do to be worthy of God's grace, rather than what God does in us and we respond to with gratitude and charity.

It is part of the genius of St. Francis that he realized the way to God is the way God came to us, not by ascending to some spiritual stratosphere, but by descending and entering our world. St. Francis's whole life was an act of thanksgiving and praise for the Gift of God, who is Jesus Christ. Francis realized the error of trying to ascend by one's own asceticism to a God who is descending while we ascend, thereby rendering futile our individualistic attempts at sanctifying our own actions.

St. Francis understood that we need to surrender to the grace of God working within us, bringing together body and soul. When the two merge in our consciousness as they are in reality, and we embrace that merging and love it, then we are on the way; and our going to heaven is as beautiful as our arriving there.

I realize that such self-acceptance, self-love, does not happen overnight. Depending on what has befallen me in life, to say "I love my whole self" may take a long time, may involve therapy, healing, another person's love and acceptance of me, and much else besides—but the point is that such self-acceptance and self-love is the goal and the beginning of any true spirituality.

For example, if I begin exploring the parameters of what I do and am as a Franciscan in the light of who I'm supposed to be and how I'm expected to act, I see that my own living of the charism of St. Francis has shrunk to shocking proportions. The moorings of my Franciscan vocation, gospel poverty, fraternity, itinerancy are exposed for what they've become in my life. Poverty is now selective "giving up" of this or that minor materiality while my whole life is really lived out in a comfortable mediocrity. I am in the middle, as it were, straddling the fence between holiness and sinfulness. Straddling may be too strong an

image for the comfortable, secure middle way I live. Fraternity has become a nominal, loose allegiance to my brothers, and itinerancy has become freedom to travel, sometimes where only those of independent means can go.

A rather harsh assessment of my life! But as I reread the sustained whine above, I see that I have slipped quite easily into the worst pitfall of the spiritual life: self-hatred and self-judgment, instead of focusing on the good God, the God of mystery and love in whose gaze I see only God's love for me and for everything created by that loving glance. I remind myself again: You do not embark on a spiritual life to discover how rotten, unworthy, ungrateful, mediocre, and imperfect you are. You walk in the footprints of Jesus and there discover how good, loving, forgiving, and prejudiced in your favor is the God who created you and sustains you. You discover or remind yourself again of how sacramental is every created thing, including you who tend to see only how far you fall beneath the goals and ideals you've set consciously or unconsciously for yourself.

Were I for only one day to compare myself with my holy father, Francis of Assisi, I would come away depressed, possibly even in a despair that would move me to abandon this vocation for some lesser image of who I can realistically become. But if I delight in having even a minimal resemblance to so great a role model, then within that tenuous comparison I begin to find that my own way of living the gospel-life resembles that of St. Francis in more ways than I suspected. St. Francis himself, when he was dying, placed his hand over the wound of Christ in his side (one of the five sacred stigmata) and said to his brothers, "I have done what was mine to do; may Christ teach you what is yours to do." There is no judgment of his brothers here; only a simple exhortation to listen to Christ, who alone can teach the brothers individually and collectively what they are to do.[8]

To be, like St. Francis, a pilgrim and stranger in this world is to acknowledge that we are not God, but that God is everywhere and that our being pilgrims and strangers means we've yet to come to that degree of openness and love that enables us to see and live the implications of a world charged with the presence of divinity. And so we feel like pilgrims and strangers moving toward an afterlife, which is union with God. What we don't see is that we are already *in* that afterlife. Life in and with God begins. The afterlife, eternity, is only the removing of the veil that keeps us from seeing what is already a reality: We live and move and have our being in God who loves us with an eternal, unconditional love.

The sacramental life of the Catholic Church is a ritualizing of the divine imminence of the transcendent God. Bread and wine, water, oil, candles, incense, consummation of married love are all external, perceivable signs of grace, of the presence of God. We are pilgrims and strangers here only in that we do not yet see and understand that this *is* our true home, that heaven is all around us, as well as where we go when we pass beyond the body into that which the body is a sign of. The body is the external configuration of our unique soul. And the leaving behind of our body (to rise again according to the Christian tradition) is the affirmation of our passing beyond the external sign into the reality that lay beneath all along.

There is in contemporary spiritual thinking and writing an increasingly positive regard for the world. The change here is clearly seen in the thinking of the Trappist Thomas Merton as he moves from his earlier to later writings. There is a most striking change in Merton's view of the world from his first book, *The Seven Storey Mountain*, to his posthumously published journal, *Dancing in the Water of Life*.

The tone of *The Seven Storey Mountain* is that Merton is leaving a wicked world to enter a sort of new Eden at Gethsemani Abbey. The world "out there" is bad while the world of "spiritual solitude" is holy—a false split again. In *Dancing in the Water of Life* an older Thomas Merton recognizes his earlier unbalanced viewpoint. He recounts a journey from Gethsemani Abbey to New York City to meet with the aging Zen Master Suzuki.

> Actually I thought I was going to hate the trip—but I loved it, and as Sandy Hook came in sight I knew what it was, immediately. Then the long string of beaches on the Jersey shore, and the twinkling water with boats in it, and dark brown hot Brooklyn and Manhattan over there. Idlewild, Kennedy Airport, enormous rumble of trucks and buildings, a vast congeries of airports, and then in the American Airlines Building fantastic beings, lovely humans, assured yet resigned, some extraordinarily beautiful, all mature and sophisticated actual people for God's sake! I had

forgotten—the tone of voice, the awareness, the weariness, the readiness to keep standing, an amazing existence, the realization of the fallible condition of man, and of the fantastic complexity of modern life.[9]

I had a similar experience on a Greyhound bus from Cincinnati, Ohio, to Florida. My first reaction to the twenty-five hour trip, by way of Lexington, Knoxville, Atlanta, and Jacksonville, was aversion and doubt that I'd last the trip. My reaction dismayed me because as a teenage seminarian I'd traveled Greyhound four times a year for the two-and-a-half-day, 1500-mile journey to and from Cincinnati and Gallup, New Mexico. In fact, I should have found the prospect of an overnight bus trip nostalgic, a return to my youth. Why, then, did I dread the trip? What happened over the years to transform my first bus ride across the United States from adventure to a distasteful burden?

Time. The acceleration of time in which I now lived. The bus took too long to get there, and in the intervening years arriving had become more important than the journey there. But once aboard the bus, pillow and Walkman in hand, and settled into a seat, I relaxed into the small world that pillow, books, tape recorder, and letting someone else drive, created. My cocoon was not unlike what many around me had made of their space, a place to read, doze, work crossword puzzles, pray, think thoughts far away from the rocking bus. The road became a monotonous tape running beneath the bus's rubber reels. I began to feel my heart calming, a quickly arrived at future replaced by a leisurely ride to the same future.

Time was one factor; the other was my fellow travelers. Somewhere between my childhood dream of following in the footsteps of St. Francis and that pivotal bus trip, I'd subtly abandoned the poor, the disenfranchised, in favor of the upper middle class, the professionals, the rich. I, who profess to be a Franciscan, shrink from the way of St. Francis, which is ever walking with the poor and those whom others find repulsive, obnoxious, or simply inconvenient. The bus trip's "epiphany" was a rediscovery of joy and peace of soul in traveling with those I would not have chosen as my companions on the way. The African-American woman across the aisle with her quiet smile, her Bible, her reaching out to help in and out of her seat another more elderly woman racked with the pain of arthritis. The young Appalachian couple with their baby and boxes roped closed in lieu of suitcases, their eyes bright with promise of something on the other side of Knoxville. The pregnant woman who smiles at me from the other side of the table at our Burger King break in London, Kentucky. The trust I gradually feel in those sitting around me, their patience, their willingness to assist those who can't lift bags into the overhead rack, those who find it difficult to go up or down the bus steps. People I'm in the habit of passing by, dismissing, on my way to yet another "important" task. Like the Jew fallen along the road in Jesus' parable of the Good Samaritan, I let myself be ministered to by those whom I initially wanted only to keep at a safe distance.

Just when I was beginning to feel like a Greyhound hermit, we reached Knoxville, and the bus filled up; an older Hispanic man sat down next to me, invading my space. I felt compelled to talk, and my solitude was broken. Others began talking with the newcomers, and what began as a cocoon of meditation ended in socializing. A not unwelcome intrusion. For silence and solitude are best broken by intervals of relaxing conversation. We were only two days away from the Thanksgiving holidays, and I imagined everyone on the bus going home for Thanksgiving. But where was home? Is home only, as Robert Frost writes in "The Death of the Hired Man," "the place where, when you have to go there,/They have to take you in"? The poet's words strip away all the illusions of home and leave us with a cold, clinical reality. We see their truth, but we hope that home is more than that. Home: hearth, safety, love, acceptance, identity. Home is where we know who we are.

I realized, seeing all these people on the bus, how domestic everything is. We're born into a family, create another family, and die identifying with an extended family that usually embraces more than the four walls of two or three houses. We grow into a sense of church, state, and even world as our family, and yet, and yet...we are also one, alone. Not lonely, but alone; for to be most alone can be to be most with others. To find God in the core of oneself is to be connected with all that is and feel an enormous compassion and love. I am one, but I am many, as well. And the more of creation that I can identify with and embrace as St. Francis did, the more whole I feel, the more integral and unique.

Chapter Three

Becoming Aware

We cannot conclude without saying something further about St. Francis and nature since it is as a lover of animals and birds that we most often imagine him. St. Francis loved all things, all creation, not as ends in themselves, but as brothers and sisters, like him, on their way to God. He used to say that "all things sing pilgrimage and exile." Everything we see and hear of ourselves and of the world around us is on pilgrimage to a new heaven and a new earth. Everything in the world is exiled from its true home.

Pilgrimage and exile may sound like strange words from one we associate with love of animals and plants, the patron saint of nature, of ecology. Strange and not so strange; for when all is said and done, St. Francis is the supreme realist, not the Romantic we sometimes make him out to be. St. Francis saw in nature an analog of the soul. Nature, like the soul, is God's vesture. It wears a garment that bespeaks its created nature. It says, "I am made, as you are made, by God's hand." It is a work that is not finished and like God's word itself it will not return empty to God.

For St. Francis, the Word of God that created all things takes on our human flesh in Jesus Christ, who by this very incarnation further sanctifies all creation. In Jesus resides not only the fullness of divinity, but in him is subsumed all of creation, as well. Earth, water, fire and air, the four cosmic elements, are not just God's creation; they are made holy by Jesus Christ in whom the elements of the universe are further sanctified. And as Jesus ascended to his true home in heaven, so all of creation will ascend one day to become a new Earth in a new heaven.

This is the thinking that informs what St. Francis is and does. He is passionately in love with Jesus Christ. He embraces all of creation as that which has been created by God's Word made tangible in Jesus. Jesus himself is the Word that speaks creation and redeems creation and summons all creation to join him in Paradise. For St. Francis, then, everything is on its way forward to heaven, backward to Paradise, the Garden of Innocence at the very beginning of creation. The trouble is, we keep mistaking things themselves, creation itself, as its own end, our heaven or Paradise. Even Earth, which we mistakenly think must be our true home, is itself a pilgrim in its way back to the Word who spoke it and redeemed it.

Franciscan spirituality has informed my own life from my thirteenth year. And though I again and again have mistaken the pilgrimage for the destination, the words of St. Francis have pulled me back from not seeing clearly enough to discern the maker from the thing made, the redeemer from the redeemed. All things do indeed sing pilgrimage and exile. And God alone is the destination.

St. Francis tells us to delight in this. He himself delights in everything, because everything is lent to us by the great and good Almsgiver. And so we rejoice not in ownership and appropriation, but in the freedom of knowing that everything we think we own and possess is really on loan from the creator, the one true God.

Francis's prayer, then, becomes a time of thanksgiving and praise of the creator, the redeemer, the savior, the one true God. And how liberating that orientation is, especially for those whose prayer time tends to become a heightened self-awareness. Awareness of the Other draws me out of self-preoccupation into the loving gaze of God whose countenance absorbs me, makes me forget my own problems or preoccupations, lost as I am in God's love. It is like the experience of falling in love, when we forget our own faults and blemishes because someone loves us, someone makes us forget about ourselves. When you love me, I see only your love for me; and in amazement that someone finds me attractive, desirable, I rise above my own doubts

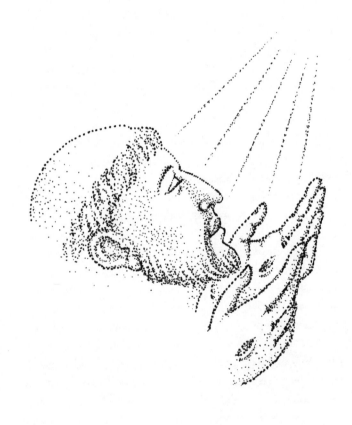

and misgivings. I become focused on you. I in turn praise your beauty, am grateful for such a gift.

This dynamic of focusing on the Other who draws me out and thereby frees me from my own limitations is the very center of what Franciscan prayer is. Spiritual exercises, silence, solitude—these are not for making me more self-conscious, but for making me aware of the one who made me, loves me, redeems me. This absorption in the Other purifies and motivates more than any self-analysis or penitential act. Examination of conscience and penance follow upon my awareness of God's love for me. They are responses to my awareness of God and consequently my own unworthiness to address God, to receive God's love. And so I try to purify my heart, knowing full well that I cannot ever be worthy of God's love. I only want to do something to show God how important God is to me and how I want to come to God as prepared and pure of heart as I can. My attempts at purification are concrete actions taken to show God (to paraphrase St. Francis) that I wish for nothing else, desire nothing else; nothing pleases and delights me but the creator, the redeemer, our savior, the one true God.

Where my gaze is, is where my heart is. Prayer is setting aside time to redirect my gaze toward the one who alone is worthy of all my attention and love. Like St. Francis, then, in reorienting my gaze, I paradoxically see everything else in a new light. St. Francis teaches me that fixing my eyes on God does not lead to contempt for created things. On the contrary, God-focus helps me to see all things as my brothers and sisters, made like me by the

Most High Good God, creatures-become-sacraments, signs of God left everywhere. That is why St. Francis praises God through, with, in, and for creation, calling them brothers and sisters.

In his *Canticle of the Creatures* St. Francis praises God through and by means of Brother Sun, the symbol of God, the source of all light; through Sister Moon and his sisters the stars, whom God has formed in the heavens bright and precious and fair. He praises God through Brother Wind and every weather by which God sustains his creatures; through Sister Water, so humble, useful, precious and chaste; through Brother Fire who lights up the night and is handsome and jocund, robust and strong; through our Sister, Mother Earth, who teaches us and feeds us with fruits and colored flowers and herbs. In short, St. Francis praises God and thanks God for everything he encounters. The place where he resides is the prayer of contemplation that moves him to praise and thanksgiving. It is this dynamic in the life of St. Francis that leads to joy, that delight in all things we associate with him.

And everything that has become defiled somehow as a result of human sin is redeemed in and through Jesus Christ, who becomes the sign and sacrament of the Most High, All-Powerful, Good God. The focus of St. Francis's life and prayer is Jesus.

In Jesus is the fullness of divinity and all creation. Jesus is the focus of St. Francis's contemplation, whether he is gazing upon a crucifix or a blade of grass. This focus, in turn, makes Francis forgetful of self, caught up as he is in Jesus who loves him and died upon the cross for him.

St. Francis prays, "May the fiery and honey-sweet power of your love, Lord, wean me from all things under heaven, so that I may die for love of your love, who deigned to die for love of my love."

The weaning St. Francis refers to is not a rejection of "all things under heaven," but a new attitude that frees him to be nourished at the breasts of God, rather than at the breasts of creation. That weaning, furthermore, creates a new valuation of all creation, which, like him, hangs upon the mercy and love of God. Our interdependence is made apparent in our dependence on God. One who loves God does not reject creation, but sees creation for what it is and loves creation as the work of God's hand. Interrelatedness, rather than separation from, is St. Francis's approach to all things. To relate well, I must fix my gaze on God, in the heavens, in my heart, in all of creation.

Thomas of Celano, St. Francis's first biographer, puts it this way.

> St. Francis praised the Artist in every one of his works; whatever he found in things made, he referred to their Maker. He rejoiced in all the works of the Lord's hands, and with joyful vision saw into the reason and cause that gave them life. In beautiful things he came to know Beauty itself. To him all things were good. They cried out to him, "He who made us is infinitely good." By tracing his footprints in things, Francis followed the Beloved wherever he led. He made, from created things, a ladder to his throne.[10]

Notes

1. Murray Bodo, O.F.M., *Through the Year with Francis of Assisi* (Cincinnati: St. Anthony Messenger Press, 1993), p. 60.

2. Karl Menninger, *The Vital Balance* (New York: Viking Press, 1963), p. 303.

3. Menninger, p. 365.

4. Bodo, p. 125.

5. Bodo, p. 82.

6. John J. L. Mood, ed., *Rilke on Love and Other Difficulties* (New York: W. W. Norton, 1975), pp. 98–99.

7. Thomas H. Johnson, ed., *The Complete Poems of Emily Dickinson* (Boston: Little, Brown, 1960), p. 153.

8. Thomas of Celano, *First Life of St. Francis*, #214, quoted in Bodo, p. 117 (Rule of 1221, Chapter XXII).

9. Thomas Merton, "The Suzuki Visit, June 16, 1964," in *Dancing in the Water of Life, The Journals of*

Thomas Merton, Vol. 5, 1963–1965, Robert E. Daggy, ed. (New York: Harpercollins, 1997), p. 114.

10. Thomas of Celano, *Second Life of St. Francis*, #165, quoted in Bodo, p. 166.

ILLUMINATIONBOOKS

Other Books in the Series

Little Pieces of Light...Darkness and Personal Growth
    by Joyce Rupp

Lessons from the Monastery That Touch Your Life
    by M. Basil Pennington, O.C.S.O.

As You and the Abused Person Journey Together
    by Sharon E. Cheston

Spirituality, Stress & You
    by Thomas E. Rodgerson

Joy, The Dancing Spirit of Love Surrounding You
    by Beverly Elaine Eanes

Every Decision You Make Is a Spiritual One
    by Anthony J. De Conciliis with John F. Kinsella

Celebrating the Woman You Are
    by S. Suzanne Mayer, I.H.M.

Why Are You Worrying?
    by Joseph W. Ciarrocchi

Partners in the Divine Dance of Our Three Person'd God
by Shaun McCarty, S.T.

Love God...Clean House...Help Others
by Duane F. Reinert, O.F.M. Cap.

Along Your Desert Journey
by Robert M. Hamma

Appreciating God's Creation Through Scripture
by Alice L. Laffey

Let Yourself Be Loved
by Phillip Bennett

Facing Discouragement
by Kathleen Fischer and Thomas Hart

Living Simply in an Anxious World
by Robert J. Wicks

A Rainy Afternoon with God
by Catherine B. Cawley

Time, A Collection of Fragile Moments
by Joan Monahan

15 Ways to Nourish Your Faith
by Susan Shannon Davies

Following in the Footsteps of Jesus
by Gerald D. Coleman, S.S. and David M. Pettingill

God Lives Next Door
by Lyle K. Weiss

Hear the Just Word & Live It
by Walter J. Burghardt, S.J.

The Love that Keeps Us Sane
by Marc Foley, O.C.D.